W9-AES-543

Pocahontas

by Shannon Zemlicka
illustrations by Jeni Reeves

On My Own
BIOGRAPHY

Carolrhoda Books, Inc./Minneapolis

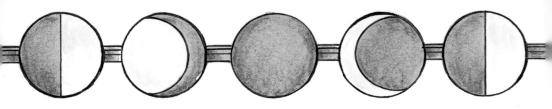

For Jill Braithwaite, a gifted mentor and treasured friend —S.Z.

For poet Yona Catron —J.R.

The illustrator would like to thank Frances Carlton and Kirk Kehrberg of the Colonial National Historic Park at Jamestown, VA, for their valuable assistance and insights.

The photograph on page 47 appears courtesy of the Virginia Historical Society.

This book is available in two editions:
Library binding by Carolrhoda Books, Inc., a division of Lerner Publishing Group
Soft cover by First Avenue Editions, an imprint of Lerner Publishing Group
241 First Avenue North
Minneapolis, MN 55401 U.S.A.

Website address: www.lernerbooks.com

Library of Congress Cataloging-in-Publication Data

Zemlicka, Shannon.
    Pocahontas / by Shannon Zemlicka ; illustrations by Jeni Reeves.
        p.   cm. — (On my own biography)
    Includes bibliographical references.
    Summary: An introduction to the life of Pocahontas, a Powhatan Indian, which covers her birth, meetings with English settlers, trip to England, family life, and death.
        ISBN: 0–87614–598–5 (lib. bdg. : alk. paper)
        ISBN: 0–87614–906–9 (pbk: alk. paper)
        1. Pocahontas, d. 1617—Juvenile literature. 2. Powhatan women—Biography—Juvenile literature. 3. Powhatan Indians—History—Juvenile literature. 4. Jamestown (Va.)—History—Juvenile literature. 5. Smith, John, 1580–1631—Juvenile literature. [1. Pocahontas, d. 1617. 2. Powhatan Indians—Biography. 3. Indians of North America—Virginia—Biography. 4. Jamestown (Va.)—History. 5. Women—Biography.] I. Reeves, Jeni, ill. II. Title. III. Series.
E99.P85 P5798 2002
975.5'01'092—dc21   2001005050

Manufactured in the United States of America
1 2 3 4 5 6 – JR – 07 06 05 04 03 02

Author's Note

Who was Pocahontas? Some people know her as a cartoon character from a movie. But she was a real person. Like all real people, Pocahontas has a true story. The trouble is, her true story is not easy to tell. Pocahontas was born more than 400 years ago. She did not write, and the people who knew her best—the Powhatan Indians—did not write either. We know her only through the writings of people who did not understand much about the Powhatans. These people came from England in the 1600s to settle the land where Pocahontas lived. That land later became known as the state of Virginia.

Did the English people who wrote down Pocahontas's story do a good job? Can we trust what they wrote? People who study the past have tried to answer these questions. By carefully reading old stories, letters, and diaries, they have learned much of Pocahontas's story. We will never know some things for sure. But the things we do know are important to remember and retell.

The village of Werowocomoco,
in what later became Virginia,
about 1595

It was a day of joy in the village.

A new baby had been born.

She was the daughter of Powhatan,

the chief of the Powhatan Indians.

Young and old gathered to celebrate

and welcome the tiny girl.

Powhatan named his daughter Matoaka.

But as she grew, she earned a nickname.

Pocahontas meant "playful one."

Most Powhatan children played a little
and worked a little.
But Pocahontas could play almost all the time.
Her family had servants to grow their food
and make their clothes.
So Pocahontas had lots of time
to explore the woods.
She had time to swim in the river.
She had time to hunt for shells
and laugh with her brothers and sisters.

In April of 1607,

life changed forever for the Powhatans.

Three ships landed on the ocean shore.

They had brought many white men.

Over the next few months, the Powhatans

watched the men from the ships.

They talked with them, too.

The men had come from England.
They had crossed the sea to reach
the Powhatans' land.
And they were building a fort!
Powhatan agreed to trade goods with the men.
But he did not trust them.

Twelve-year-old Pocahontas
was curious about the English.
What did they look like?
How did they live?
That winter,
she had a chance to find out.

In January of 1608, Pocahontas went
to a feast at her father's longhouse.
There she saw an English man
called Captain John Smith.
He had gone too far into Powhatan's land
and been taken prisoner.
John Smith was a strange-looking person.
His hair was yellow and grew all over his face.
Powhatan talked about killing the intruder.
But Pocahontas spoke up.
She asked her father not to kill John Smith.
Then two large stones were brought in.
John Smith's head was placed on them.
Powhatan's men raised their clubs.
Pocahontas ran to John Smith.
She covered him with her body.
Powhatan stopped the men.
John Smith would not be killed.

Many years later, Smith wrote that
Pocahontas had saved his life that day.
But it may not really have happened at all.
Smith liked to brag about his adventures.
And he did not tell the story until
many years after that night.
Some people who study the past
think that Smith made up the story.
Others think he did not understand
what happened to him.
Powhatan may have been leading a ceremony
to make Smith one of his people.
He may have just pretended to kill Smith
as part of the ceremony.
Pocahontas and the men with clubs
may have been pretending, too.

John Smith was allowed to return
to Jamestown, the English fort.
That winter was hard on the English.
A fire burned parts of Jamestown.
The people had little shelter or food.

Powhatan decided to help.

He sent Pocahontas to the English.

Servants went with her,

carrying baskets of bread and meat.

The English would have starved

without this food.

For a while, the Powhatans and the English

got along well.

But by the spring,

they were fighting about trading.

Each side took prisoners.

Powhatan sent his daughter with a message.

Would John Smith release

his Indian prisoners?

Smith said yes.

Because Pocahontas had come,

he would let the prisoners go.

Pocahontas kept visiting
Jamestown that summer.
She even went when Powhatan
did not send her.
There was so much to see and do there!
The men gave her presents,
like pretty beads and a mirror.

No girls lived in Jamestown yet,
but the English boys were fun to play with.
They turned cartwheels in the marketplace
and played games.
Pocahontas talked often with John Smith, too.
She taught him some Powhatan words.
He helped her learn to speak English.

That fall, Pocahontas became good friends
with the English.

She liked John Smith best of all.

But her father was not so sure

he liked the English.

They were exploring more and more
of the land he ruled.

They were making friends with Indians
who were enemies of the Powhatans.

They demanded corn even when
the Powhatans had none to trade.

Were they planning to take land, too?

At last, Powhatan made up his mind.

He would act to protect his people.

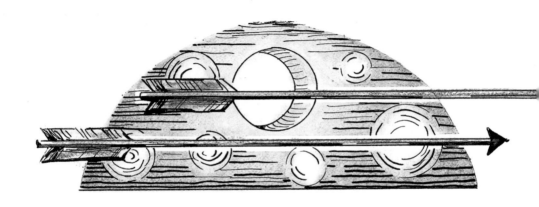

A Warning
January 13, 1609

Faster!

Pocahontas ran and ran.

She must go faster!

She had learned something terrible.

Her father was planning to kill John Smith!

Smith was visiting Werowocomoco to trade.

Powhatan was going to surprise him.

Pocahontas knew that her father had

good reasons to fear the English.

But to her, they were friends.

She had to warn them.

At last, Pocahontas reached the longhouse
where the English were staying.
She told John Smith about Powhatan's plan.
She did not know it,
but John Smith had plans, too.
He wanted to capture Powhatan
and steal all his corn.
John thanked Pocahontas.

He tried to give her some beads.
Pocahontas shook her head
and started to cry.
Didn't he know what would happen
if her father saw her with those beads?
Powhatan would know what she had done.
He might have *her* killed.

John Smith returned to Jamestown.
The English and the Powhatans
began fighting.
Pocahontas still visited Jamestown
when she could.
But later that year, the English told her
something awful.
John Smith had died.
As another winter settled over Virginia,
Pocahontas felt heavy with grief.
She was sure that her dear friend
was lost to her forever.

Prisoner of the English
April 1613

Pocahontas clenched her fists.

She could hardly believe

what had happened to her.

She was back at Jamestown.

But this time, she was a prisoner.

For more than four years, the fighting

between the Powhatans

and the English had continued.

Pocahontas had grown into a young woman.

All this time, she had stayed away

from Jamestown.

Then the English captured her.

The friends she had helped so many times

were holding her for ransom.

They wanted Powhatan to trade English

prisoners and guns for his daughter.

After a few weeks, Powhatan sent

the prisoners and some guns.

He promised to send corn after the harvest.

But Pocahontas was not allowed to leave.

She was sent to Henrico,

another English town.

There, a minister began to teach her.

Pocahontas practiced speaking English.

She learned about the Christian religion.
The women of Henrico dressed her
like an English lady.
She wore huge, heavy skirts.
Fabric covered her from her neck to her feet.
Instead of spending her days outside
like a Powhatan woman,
Pocahontas sat still in a house.

Pocahontas learned quickly.

One of her teachers, John Rolfe,

saw that she was eager and smart.

As months passed,

he fell in love with Pocahontas.

He asked her to marry him.

Pocahontas agreed.

Did she love John Rolfe?

No one knows for sure.

The English who knew them thought so.

But Pocahontas was still a prisoner.

She may have had other reasons to marry.

Maybe she wanted a little more freedom.

Maybe she wanted a home of her own.

Before the wedding, English leaders
took Pocahontas to see Powhatan.
They still hoped to collect ransom for her.
It was March of 1614.
Pocahontas had been a prisoner
for almost a year.
Two of Pocahontas's brothers met them.
But her father did not come.

Pocahontas was hurt.

Was her father afraid of the English?

Or did he just want to keep his guns?

If Powhatan loved guns

more than he loved her,

she would stay with the English, she said.

Then she told her brothers that she wanted

to marry John Rolfe.

Later, Powhatan sent a message
to Jamestown.
He said that Pocahontas could
marry John Rolfe.
And he would send the guns and corn
the English wanted.
He wanted his daughter to be happy,
and he wanted to make peace
with the English.
Around this time,
Pocahontas was baptized as a Christian.
She was given a new name, Lady Rebecca.
Rebecca's teachers boasted that she
had given up her beliefs for theirs.
But no one knows what she thought.
Rebecca may have held her Powhatan life
close to her heart,
even as she began an English life.

In April of 1614, Rebecca married John Rolfe.

They moved to a house of their own.

Several Powhatan women came

to serve Rebecca and keep her company.

The next year,

she gave birth to a son, Thomas.

Was Rebecca happy?

No one knows.

But because of her marriage, a time of peace
began for the Powhatans and the English.

It was called the Peace of Pocahontas.

London, England, 1616

Rebecca gazed at the crowd.

Her eyes grew wide with wonder.

She had never seen anything like London.

Thousands of people swarmed

through the streets.

The city stank of smoke, trash,

and human waste.

Virginia's leaders had sent Rebecca
and her family here.
A few Powhatans also made the journey.
They were helping raise money
for the Virginia settlements.
London was nothing like home.
But Rebecca found things to love anyway.
In London, she was famous.

No one there had ever met
an Indian chief's daughter,
especially not a Christian one.
Rebecca went to parties and plays.
Handsome lords and beautiful ladies
became her friends.
She even met the king and queen
of England.

But London was not fun for long.

The air was damp and smoky, so different

from the fresh air of Virginia's forests.

Diseases spread quickly.

Several of the Powhatan travelers got sick.

Some died.

And sometime during her stay,

Rebecca heard shocking news.

Her old friend John Smith

was not dead after all!

He was alive—and in England!

Why had he not come to see her?

Before Rebecca could find out,

she got sick too.

John Rolfe moved his family

to the town of Brentford.

The air was better there.

At Brentford, John Smith came to visit
the Rolfes at last.
Rebecca was shocked to see him at her door.
Here was the friend she had trusted.
She had brought him food
when he was starving.
She had taught him her language.
She had tried to protect him from her father.
How could he have ignored her
all these years?
Rebecca had only angry words for John Smith.
Their talk must not have helped her.
She grew sicker and weaker.
John Rolfe decided to bring her home
to Virginia.
But she was too sick to sail so far.
The Rolfes stopped their ship to rest
in the town of Gravesend.

Rebecca realized that she would die.

She was only about 21 years old.

But she told John that she did not mind.

Everyone dies, she said.

It was good enough for her

that their son was still alive.

Rebecca died in March of 1617.

The next year,

the Peace of Pocahontas ended.

Afterword

It's frustrating not to know the whole truth about Pocahontas. Did she really save John Smith's life? Why did she marry John Rolfe? Even though she left behind many unanswered questions, people have always wanted to tell stories about her. Some people may not have told the truth, and some made mistakes in what they told. Along the way, the real Pocahontas got lost.

If we want to tell Pocahontas's true story, we have to accept that there are things we don't know about her. But we can still remember and share the things we do know about Pocahontas. We know that she was a curious, intelligent person who played an important part in American history. She helped the Jamestown settlers survive their difficult first years. Later, her marriage brought about years of peace between the Powhatans and the English. In the earliest days of the English settlements that later grew into the United States, Pocahontas lived as a bridge between two worlds.

Important Dates

1595?—Pocahontas is born in what later becomes
Virginia. (Her exact date of birth is not known.)

1607—English settlers begin building Jamestown in
Powhatan territory.

1608—Pocahontas meets John Smith; brings food to
Jamestown; helps arrange release of prisoners

1609—Warns John Smith of her father's plan to attack
him

1613—Is taken prisoner by the English and held at
Jamestown and Henrico; is taught English
manners and the Christian religion; meets John
Rolfe

1614—Is baptized as a Christian; name is changed to
Rebecca; marries John Rolfe

1615—Birth of son, Thomas

1616—Travels to London, England, with family

1617—Dies in Gravesend, England

Selected Bibliography

Barbour, Philip. *The Complete Works of Captain John Smith, vols. 1-3.*
Chapel Hill, NC: University of North Carolina Press, 1986.

Barbour, Philip. *Pocahontas and Her World.* Boston: Houghton Mifflin, 1970.

Gleach, Frederic W. *Powhatan's World and Colonial Virginia: A Conflict
of Culture.* Lincoln, NE: University of Nebraska Press, 1997.

Hamor, Ralph. *A True Discourse of the Present State of Virginia.* 1615.
Reprint, Richmond, VA: Virginia State Library, 1957.

Harriot, Thomas. *A Briefe and True Report of the New Found Land of
Virginia.* 1590. Reprint, with an introduction by Paul Hulton, New
York: Dover Publications, Inc., 1972.

Rountree, Helen C. *Pocahontas's People.* Norman, OK: University of
Oklahoma Press, 1990.

Rountree, Helen C. *The Powhatan Indians of Virginia.* Norman, OK:
University of Oklahoma Press, 1989.